Original title:
Rooms of Silence

Copyright © 2025 Creative Arts Management OÜ
All rights reserved.

Author: Levi Montgomery
ISBN HARDBACK: 978-1-80587-035-7
ISBN PAPERBACK: 978-1-80587-505-5

Shadows Beneath Stillness

In corners where echoes of laughter reside,
The dust bunnies dance, oh, what a wild ride!
The cat steals a glance, then lays down with a sigh,
While old chairs compete in a bendy old bye.

Hushed Corners of the Heart

The toaster hums softly, awaiting its dues,
While socks plot revenge, in mismatched hues.
A sleepy old clock ticks its lullabies sweet,
While the fridge hums a tune, tapping its feet.

Abandoned Spaces of Thought

Under the bed, where that sock monster resides,
Are ideas long lost, with nowhere to hide.
A film of dust gathers, on thoughts left unchecked,
They giggle and whisper, seeking respect.

The Quietude of Forgotten Places

In every nook where daydreams go to play,
The past holds court, insisting it'll stay.
Mice scurry with secrets, a chuckle they share,
While the shadows conspire, just floating in air.

Untold Stories in the Silence

In the quiet, cats plot schemes,
While socks escape in moonlit dreams.
Dust bunnies whisper tales of old,
As secrets gather, bold yet cold.

Lamps flicker, trying their best,
To light up stories and jest.
Coffee cups in stillness sway,
Laughing at the words we say.

Tranquil Spaces of Reflection

There's an echo of a sneeze,
As thoughts bounce back like summer breeze.
Chairs creak and giggles spark,
In corners where shadows embark.

Mirrors chuckle at our hair,
Framing faces with little care.
The fridge hums a low, sweet tune,
As leftovers join the quiet festoon.

The Sound of Silent Moments

Tick-tock steals the breath away,
Time plays games in a sneaky way.
Peeking through the gaps of night,
Are whispers turned to pure delight.

Keyboards click with full-on sass,
While mice scurry, seeking grass.
Even clocks can slip and slide,
Creating moments we can't abide.

Silent Witnesses of Time

Books stacked high with a knowing grin,
Comics blush, where tales begin.
Piles of laundry dream and sigh,
As dust settles—oh, my my!

Old shoes chuckle on the floor,
Reminding us they've walked before.
Underneath the quiet air,
Lies a riot with stories rare.

The Beauty of Unexpressed Thoughts

In corners deep, thoughts start to stew,
Bottled up laughter, the jokes that won't do.
Muffled giggles try to sneak and escape,
They wiggle and dance, but can't find their shape.

Ideas collide like socks in the wash,
They tumble and twist, creating a nosh.
Whispers of hilarity behind closed doors,
Like secretive meetings of squirrel explorers.

The Space Between Each Breath

Each inhale tickles, a giggle in disguise,
Exhales release chuckles, oh how time flies.
Moments hang heavy, like fruit on a vine,
Waiting to drop, but not quite in line.

A breath caught midway, a hiccup of glee,
Laughter bubbles up, just shy of a spree.
In the pause, there's magic, a fun little break,
Where silence plays tricks, and all senses quake.

Silence, a Gentle Caress

Quiet moments, they tickle the air,
A soft, sweet touch, just like a fair.
It blankets the room in playful disguise,
Stifled snickers sneak, oh what a surprise!

Laughter on the edge, never quite said,
Like a garden of giggles, just waiting instead.
The hush holds its breath, ready to tease,
Creating a ruckus with mischievous ease.

Lighthouses Guarding the Unsaid

Tall beacons glimmer in the night's embrace,
Guiding lost giggles through a thoughtful space.
They shine on the shores of what's left unheard,
With a wink and a grin, they coax out a word.

Each flicker of light holds secrets so bright,
Like moths to a flame, they dance with delight.
The stories untold, wrapped tight in the mist,
Waiting to burst forth, a comedic twist.

Forgotten Mirrors of Reflection

In corners where dust bunnies groove,
Mirrors hang, holding secrets to prove.
Each smudge a whisper, a giggle or two,
Reflecting the chaos in shades of blue.

The cat strikes a pose, then slips on a shoe,
A tale of proportions, oh what a view!
Grandmas in aprons shake their heads slow,
While pickles throw parties, though no one will know.

The Weight of Unuttered Words

Words float around like balloons on a string,
Pockets of silence, yet laughter they bring.
A knock at the door, a spout full of cheer,
But nobody answers, they're all out of beer.

Conversations delayed by an awkward sigh,
Who knew the fridge had such a sly eye?
The weight of the silence, a sandwich so bold,
It dreams of a toast that's been left in the cold.

A Galaxy of Empty Spaces

Empty spaces are groovin' like stars in the night,
The couch does the cha-cha, what a silly sight!
A galaxy spins where no dust ever lands,
And socks argue fiercely about who makes the plans.

The fridge is a comet that goes on a spree,
Chasing leftovers in a cosmic decree.
A universe forms 'neath the clutter we tread,
And laughter ignites like old toast that's been fed.

Where Time Pauses to Listen

Tick-tock, there's a gopher with stories to share,
A clock in the corner, with much wisdom to spare.
Time takes a seat, in a soft, squishy chair,
Munching on popcorn, with nary a care.

Boredom's a jester, but giggles abound,
As potted plants sway, talking sacred ground.
Every tick is a chuckle, a tickle of fate,
As whispers of mischief from shadows await.

Whispers in Abandoned Halls

In a house where shadows play,
Dust bunnies dance in dismay.
Empty chairs tell stories bold,
Of wild parties now grown old.

Silent echoes laugh and creep,
While the walls discreetly weep.
Forgotten socks on the floor,
Whisper secrets of yore.

Ghosts of laughter float around,
Chasing echoes in the sound.
A fridge hums a sleepy tune,
While the cat assumes the moon.

Once in a while, a creak will tease,
Is that a ghost, or just the breeze?
In this quiet, silly space,
We find joy in empty grace.

Echoes of Solitude

In corners where the sun won't peek,
A lonely chair begins to squeak.
Plates of dust on a table stand,
Challenging reality's bland.

The fridge has secrets, oh so deep,
Of ancient leftovers now in sleep.
A sock escapes from laundry's clutch,
Who knew silence could mean so much?

A spider weaves a web of dreams,
While sunlight dances, and the room beams.
Ticking clocks with jokes to tell,
In this quiet, all's quite well.

Toys lying low begin to sigh,
Why's the cat the only one so spry?
Here, in stillness, fun's the game,
In every shadow, laughter's name.

The Quiet Corners of Being

In nooks where whispers softly land,
Laughter echoes, but it's quite bland.
The dust motes twirl in a dance,
While the old chair gives a knowing glance.

Socks of specters play hide and seek,
With echoes of laughter on the peak.
The vacuum cleaner takes a break,
Nibbling crumbs from a peanut cake.

Potted plants compete for a grin,
Their leaves rustle gently; let's begin!
In this shelter of quiet cheer,
Giggles and grins seem to appear.

The cat sprawls out with perfect ease,
Stealing a nap, not caring, just breeze.
In corners quiet, joy does loom,
Life's a jest in every room.

Stillness Beneath the Surface

Beneath the calm, there's mischief near,
A sneaky mouse could disappear.
When no one's watching, walls will talk,
And in the silence, laughter walks.

Stuck beans under sofa's reign,
Whisper tales of joy and pain.
The clock tick-tocks with funny quirks,
Counting moments where silliness lurks.

A picture frame's upside-down cheer,
Shows a cat that once loved a deer.
Every shadow plays the fool,
In this silence, fun's the rule.

The curtains sway in a subtle plot,
Hatching giggles, a bubbling thought.
Here, beneath the muted glow,
We find laughter in the flow.

Veils of Unspoken Thoughts

In corners where whispers quirk,
Dust bunnies reside and smirk.
A sock lost here, a shoe found there,
Silent conversations fill the air.

The cat gives a judgmental glare,
As I talk to the chair with flair.
A tango between me and the wall,
Echoing laughter with no one at all.

Mismatched socks join in the jest,
As I ponder which one's the best.
A wardrobe creaks, it knows the score,
Jokes unshared, still laughter's roar.

Invisible friends share a drink,
In silent rooms where we all think.
Peeking through the cracks of light,
Quirky shadows dance in the night.

The Sound of Dust Settling

In the attic where old dreams lay,
Dust settles in a cheeky display.
A moth flutters by, a dance of glee,
Who needs a party? Just you and me!

Old records spin tales of the past,
Each scratch brings laughter, shadows cast.
A misplaced broom with legs to run,
Even chores can have a bit of fun!

The creaking floorboards sing a tune,
To the rhythm of a lazy afternoon.
A clock watches, with no time to keep,
In this quiet place, we silently leap.

Boxes stacked high, secrets they keep,
While we giggle in a pile, half asleep.
A sigh from the cat, an exasperated sound,
In this world of dust, joy abounds!

Specters of Unheard Dreams

In the hall where shadows play,
Dreams float gently, whisked away.
Invisible figures dance and prance,
Caught in a chuckle, lost in a chance.

A mirror giggles, reflecting old styles,
As whispers trade sarcastic smiles.
The carpet rolls out a punny tale,
While the couch sighs, refusing to bail.

Light creeps softly, peeking around,
Confetti of thoughts strewn on the ground.
A napkin scribbled with hopes long due,
Echoing laughter, oh, who knew?

Ghosts of visions, playful and spry,
In the corners, they tease and sigh.
Where dreams once whispered, now it's a spree,
In this comic ballet, it's just you and me!

Breaths Caught in Faded Light

Under the lamp where shadows invite,
The surreal comedy of mixed delight.
An old shoe squeaks a silly refrain,
While dust dances like it's in the rain.

Chairs join forces for a gossip spree,
As I debate with an old TV.
Each flicker of the screen, a joke told,
In the glow, colorful tales unfold.

Echoes of laughter slide through the air,
A hilarity hidden everywhere.
The fridge hums softly, it's in on the fun,
As leftovers plot to unite as one.

The window chuckles, frames a sight,
Of wandering cats in the fading light.
In a world where whimsy always thrives,
The silence jests; oh, how it revives!

Unwritten Pages of the Soul

In corners where dust bunnies dwell,
Invisible laughter begins to swell.
A cat naps loud, it's quite a charade,
While echoes of secrets are neatly laid.

Don't mind the shadows, they dance quite well,
Choreographed whispers with stories to tell.
A chair with a blanket, a soft little throne,
Where the echo of thoughts is forever alone.

The clock ticks softly, its fate is a tease,
Time's foolish prank, it's all just a breeze.
Once a place of chatter, ideas aglow,
Now it's a stage where silence can flow.

Yet in this stillness, humor takes flight,
Like socks on the ceiling, a comical sight.
With each unwritten page, absurdity sings,
As laughter and silence are curious things.

Reverberations in a Silent Room

The walls hold their breath, not a sound around,
But the squeaks and the creaks make a weird little sound.
A sneeze breaks the quiet, what a charming commotion,
It echoes and lingers—such awkward devotion.

A dust mote's ballet in a sunbeam's embrace,
Turns a calm sanctuary into a wild chase.
A ghost with a giggle, I swear I can hear,
Slips through the silence, it's hilariously near.

Chairs shuffle softly when no one is there,
Perhaps they're discussing the latest hot air.
A table that teeters on secrets so bright,
Cracks jokes with a candlestick all through the night.

When whispers get tangled, they form into knots,
The comical chaos reverts into thoughts.
In echoes that bounce, silliness blooms,
As laughter reverberates in all quiet rooms.

Ghost Lights in a Shuttered Window

Curtains drawn tight, yet shadows play peek,
Flickering flashbacks, they tickle and sneak.
A light bulb hangs low as if in a trance,
While the dust on the shelf puts up its own dance.

Shuttered views filter thoughts from the past,
Whispers of specters who think they can last.
They giggle in glimmers, a mischievous band,
As chairs start to wobble at their ghostly command.

What's that? A chuckle? A light-hearted sigh?
An empty old room can still aim for the sky.
With beams that go wobbly and flickers that spin,
The humor's contagious, it draws you right in!

So here in the shadows, we'll toast with a grin,
To the lights in the darkness that whirl from within.
With laughter like lanterns in this silent night,
Ghost lights have claimed laughter as their true delight.

The Weight of Words Never Spoke

Beneath the whispers where thoughts go to hide,
The weight of the silence starts giggling inside.
Page after page of blank stares abound,
Yet thoughts tickle toes that dance on the ground.

Unsaid conversations float thick in the air,
A cacophony of nothing; it's quite a rare flair.
With views that are silent, absurdly profound,
Each word left unsaid makes a comical sound.

The couch holds its breath, it's pulling a prank,
As unspoken laughter fills the quiet tank.
Here intentions collide, like socks in a wash,
A symphony of silence begins as a nosh.

In this weight of the unvoiced, humor takes charge,
As silence turns sagas into something quite large.
So here's to the things that we never could say,
They dance in the stillness, they humor our play.

Beneath the Quiet Surface

In shadows where the whispers creep,
A cat sits snug in a quiet heap.
The pasta boils, the clock's on pause,
And silence sneezes, with great applause.

The chairs hold secrets, strong and stout,
Where laughter tried to sneak about.
The tea's gone cold, but who would care?
A sock's gone rogue, in the kitchen chair.

The fridge hums soft, a tune so sly,
It knows the snacks the blue sky can't buy.
And in the corner, dust bunnies dance,
While the remote's lost, given the chance.

Oh, underneath this tranquil guise,
A plate of cookies just rolled its eyes.
But when the doorbell rings, what a thrill,
Let's see whose face is crowned with chill!

The Pulse of Unshared Secrets

A door ajar, a secret's glee,
Hiding the noise of an old TV.
The curtains flutter like they know,
That even silence has a show.

A dusty chair with tales to tell,
While sneakers hide and sprout their smell.
The floorboards creak, they join the fun,
With every step, they're on the run.

A ghost of laughter fills the air,
With whispers of who's sitting where.
The clocks are stuck in a tappy race,
Tick-tock, tick-tock, oh what a space!

Yet in this nook where silence swirls,
There's always room for awkward twirls.
A mug that's chipped gives a wink,
Promises of tea that made us think!

Breathing in Absence

The air is thick, it's got a joke,
Like socks that wander and never croak.
The light above flickers with glee,
A dance of shadows for eyes to see.

The table's set for an empty heart,
Where crumbs collect, a work of art.
A joke books waits, but not a chuckle,
As dust settles, it starts to snuggle.

Behind closed doors, the laughter's shy,
With echoes of jokes floating by.
The floor may sigh with a creak or two,
While the fridge hums back, in quiet stew.

Oh, what a place, this hushy club,
With a rubber chicken, the last stub!
We breathe in absence, giggles unfurl,
In this soft corner of a silly swirl!

Broken Echoes in Twilight

The twilight whispers, a playful tease,
A sock's lost course brings us to our knees.
Where shadows misbehave and giggle bold,
Tales of oops and owies unfold.

A chair asks, 'Will you take a seat?'
Ignoring me, it's still so sweet.
As paper planes soar through the gloom,
Leaving behind the scent of perfume.

The clock takes a break from ticking time,
Playing hopscotch with a nursery rhyme.
In every corner, a mirthful glance,
Where the broomsticks gather for a dance.

In this house of quirks, where giggles bloom,
The echoes crackle, filling the room.
With twilight's charm, it's all a game,
Here's to the quiet, never the same!

A Lament for Voices Lost

In a space where echoes play,
Muffled laughter drifts away.
I swear I heard a joke so grand,
But here it slips right through my hand.

The chairs all creak in soft delight,
As shadows dance in pale moonlight.
I miss the banter, was it neat?
Or was it just the sound of feet?

A cockatoo squawks, but it's mute,
With every chirp, it seems to hoot.
With voices lost, my mirth takes flight,
Yet silence reigns, oh what a sight!

What tales should I have faintly known?
Weird stories, whispers, all alone.
Instead, I sit and rue the cost,
Of lively chats forever lost.

Fragments of Distant Conversations

A murmur drifts across the room,
Like cactus blooms where shadows loom.
My ears catch whispers, soft and meek,
On topics strange, yet far too bleak.

The walls conspire, oh what a scheme,
To hold on tight to each lost dream.
Was that a rant on socks or hats?
Or something wild 'bout acrobats?

Giggles spin like silk in air,
Yet I am left with just despair.
The fragile threads, they fray and break,
I'll never know what's at stake.

With missing words, I craft my plot,
Innuendos in the perfect spot.
If only I could catch the tone,
But now I talk to plants, alone.

Whispers in the Void

In the void where giggles used to bloom,
Each silence settles like dust in a room.
I squint at shadows with hopeful sighs,
As crickets plot their grand disguise.

Who knew that hush could be so loud?
A rubber chicken lost in a crowd.
I hear the tumble of words misplaced,
With laughter trailing like confetti laced.

The air is thick with jokes untold,
While muted voices grow so bold.
But here I sit, a lone hyena,
Snickering still at an unseen diva.

In this place where chatter decays,
I weave tales in the oddest ways.
With every pause, the fun's hard to find,
Yet I chuckle loud, alone in my mind.

The Echo Chamber of Dreams

In chambers bright with laughter trapped,
The thoughts of jesters lie collapsed.
I knock on walls, what do I hear?
But blowing winds and whispered cheer.

"Knock, knock," I shout, "who's there tonight?"
An echo answers, "Just take flight."
As if the moon has grown a grin,
And hides the mischief deep within.

I've caught the muse in silent jest,
A rubber duck in formal dress.
With every baffle, joy takes hold,
In the chamber's depth, where dreams unfold.

So here I laugh, while voices stray,
Through echoes bright that choose to play.
And though the sound may flee the scene,
In merry silence, I am keen.

Dark Corners of the Heart

In the corner, emotions dance,
A waltz of socks and mismatched pants.
Whispers echo, a silly cheer,
While dust bunnies plot without a fear.

Secrets crawl like ants on a spree,
With giggles hiding behind a tree.
Beneath the bed, a lost shoe waits,
What's that? Oh dear, it's my fate!

Each sigh collects like pages torn,
Setting the mood for a laugh or scorn.
Chasing shadows, the heart takes flight,
In corners dark, there's joy in the night.

So raise a cup to the quiet tunes,
Where chaos blends with clumsy moves.
To laughter hiding in burst of cries,
In funny places, the heart defies.

The Space Where Voices Fade

Hushed giggles in the corners play,
As shadows stretch to steal the day.
Silly echoes when no one's here,
Just me and my thoughts, oh dear, oh dear!

Whispers slip like ice on a floor,
"Was that a shout?" I can't ignore!
A clever cat, a sleepy dog,
Murmur secrets in a cozy fog.

Invisible jokes hang in the air,
Tickling silence with feathered flair.
What's that? A sneeze, or a snort,
In the space where nonsense is sport.

So let the quiet be our jest,
In this silence, we can rest.
With a chuckle, we'll hide our glee,
In this hush, just you and me.

A Contrast of Dusk and Dawn

Dawn cracks open with sleepy cheer,
As dusk giggles, "I'll see you here!"
The sun yawns, gives night a wink,
Where shadows sway and candles blink.

Napping thoughts in the hazy light,
Frolic in dreams that take to flight.
In laughter's arms, both day and night,
Where silence sparkles, oh what a sight!

Winks and nudges in the twilight's glow,
Dusk says, "Tomorrow, let's take it slow."
While dawn playfully shakes the dew,
And mumbles jokes only we knew.

So here's to the giggles that blend and sway,
A merry dance at the end of the day.
Between the silly and serious,
Life finds a way to be delirious!

Dusty Tomes of the Unheard

Books stacked high in eager rows,
Whispering tales of silly woes.
The dust bunnies giggle, a happy choir,
As their stories swirl in a dusty mire.

Pages flutter like playful birds,
"Read us please!" they chirp in words.
Hidden tales of laughter bold,
Where secrets lurk and dreams unfold.

Between the lines, a joke resides,
In chapters where the truth hides.
A twisty plot, a hiccup here,
As dusty tomes cheer for those who dare.

So grab a book, let laughter rise,
In silence where the wisdom lies.
For in the quiet, we cleverly play,
In dusty tomes, we find our way.

Vows Made in the Still

In corners where the dust bunnies play,
Two chairs gossip on a lazy day.
They bond over crumbs, a collected feast,
While the old fridge hums, a hungry beast.

A cat strolls through, tail held high,
Curious about the secrets nearby.
Whiskers twitch in the light's soft glow,
As laughter echoes from the floors below.

Piles of laundry form a fortress tall,
Where socks conspire to make a great call.
They plot their escape, the great unknown,
While the couch snores on, proud and alone.

So here we sit, in this quiet mirth,
A comedy played on the stage of earth.
With every creak, a joke of sorts,
In the stillness, laughter's spirit cavorts.

The Unvoiced Stories Within Walls

Walls wear thin tales, they chuckle and sigh,
Invisible jesters that float up high.
When the clock strikes twelve, secrets spill forth,
In whispers of mischief, they show their worth.

A picture hangs crooked, with a smirk so sly,
While the stale air bursts with a faint lye.
The floorboards dance, each squeak a refrain,
Sharing old stories, a humorous gain.

Potted plants roll their eyes at the air,
As they witness the antics of chairs in despair.
The curtains chuckle at the sun's bright glee,
Eavesdropping on the jokes spelled out for free.

In this sanctuary, the laughter's a buzz,
Echoing life, the way only home does.
And though words are few, the humor is rich,
In unvoiced tales, we find our niche.

Fleeting Moments of Abandonment

Once an umbrella, now a lost cause,
Left behind, escaping the rain's applause.
A shoe on the doorstep, lonely as dawn,
Wonders if its partner has merrily gone.

A forgotten sandwich, quite past its prime,
Sits in delight at its new lease on time.
The smelly socks giggle in scented retreat,
As the dust bunnies dance to a stale beat.

Old postcards murmur from a cluttered drawer,
Remembering travels to places galore.
While the lamp flickers, casting silly shadows,
Casting doubts about the wisdom of meadows.

So raise a toast to all things left behind,
In the corner of laughter, we easily find.
Those fleeting moments, they keep us alive,
With joy in abandonment, we strive and thrive.

Silhouettes of Old Whispers

The lamp throws shadows, a curious dance,
As furniture whispers of fate and chance.
They share giggles, the tales of the night,
While the clock keeps ticking, with no end in sight.

In a forgotten nook, the dust motes play,
In games of hide and seek, they lead astray.
The old rug chuckles, embracing the scene,
As tangled thoughts wrap around the serene.

Under the table, a rogue crumb in glee,
Knows it's the king of its own tiny spree.
And the curtains sway with grandiosity,
Showing off secrets, a fine curiosity.

In these silhouettes, laughter unfolds,
With every whisper, a story retold.
A symphony brewed in the still of the night,
Where shadows sing praise to the silly delight.

When Time Hangs in Quiet Grace

In a corner sits a chair,
Where dust bunnies dance without a care,
Tick-tock whispers on the wall,
While socks have their fun, having a ball.

The cat sprawls wide, claiming the light,
Sunbeams tickle him, oh what a sight,
He dreams of chasing things he can't see,
Maybe fish or a tree, who knows, not me!

A clock takes a nap, it's running late,
While chairs have a gossip 'bout the food on a plate,
Fridge hums a tune like a poet's sweet rhyme,
Even the carpet enjoys sipping on time.

So here's to the laughter, the stillness we find,
In these quirky corners of the human mind,
Where silence can giggle and moments do tease,
And time hangs in grace like a soft summer breeze.

Hidden Sanctuaries of the Mind

Behind a closed door, ideas play leap,
The toaster winks, making bread sing deep,
Thoughts tumble around, like confetti in air,
While shoes plan their trip, with nary a care.

Whispers of coffee pots brewing a joke,
While quiet notebooks just smile and poke,
The lamp flickers light, casting shadows anew,
As thoughts wander wild, oh, how they pursue!

Cushions debate on who gets the fun,
Remote controls hang, too lazy to run,
The fridge avoids drama, keeps secrets on ice,
In this hidden retreat, where time rolls like dice.

So let's gather laughter, in corners unseen,
Where silence is quirky and slightly obscene,
In places imagined, let nonsense unwind,
In the secretive layers of the curious mind.

Awash in Still Waters

There's a pond in the mind, so calm and so clear,
Where ducks quack puns, inducing a cheer,
The goldfish swim circles, such graceful ballet,
While dragonflies laugh, and sunbeams play.

Ripples of thought, they giggle with glee,
A canoe drifts by, paddled by a bee,
The frogs sing a mix of old-fashioned tunes,
Floating on lily pads, beneath lazy moons.

As bubbles rise up, they joke on their way,
Each pop a reminder—a blooper replay,
The shadows sit down for a raucous debate,
With reflections and giggles, they all congregate.

In stillness we find, like poets in flight,
Awash in the waters, the humor is bright,
So let's splash around in this delightful dream,
Where silence is funny and thoughts make us beam.

Starlit Thoughts in Stillness

When stars decide to take a short nap,
They twinkle and chuckle in celestial chap,
The moon just grins, playing hide and seek,
While comets toss jokes, like a cheeky sneak.

Clouds whisper tales in the night's gentle sigh,
While planets toss confetti, oh my, oh my,
Galaxies giggle, in cosmic delight,
As silence wraps softly around the night.

Asteroids tumble, chatting about fate,
While black holes munch snacks, joining this state,
A shooting star scoffs, "Do I need a wish?"
As laughter falls down, in this ever-so-sweet dish.

So in the deep stillness where starlit thoughts lay,
Let's gather the humor and play every day,
For silence can chuckle while gently it sways,
In the depths of the cosmos, our laughter plays.

Breathless in the Still Air

When the cat naps on the chair,
And we tiptoe like a thief,
An accidental sneeze will flare,
Turning calm to comic grief.

Dust bunnies dance, a secret play,
While we giggle, hand on mouth,
What games they have, unplanned ballet,
As we whisper shushes, no doubt.

Hours drift by, like a joke unwound,
A salad of quiet, with laughter inside,
In the stillness, absurdity found,
In the air, where silence resides.

We discover socks and a sock puppet,
Unspoken puns float in the breeze,
In the calm, let humor erupt it,
As we wrestle with whispered wheezes.

Reflections in a Dim Light

In the half-light, shadows play,
Like two clowns in a tiny room,
They prance and sway without delay,
While lampshades wiggle, creating gloom.

A misplaced spoon bounces with glee,
As the fridge hums a jazzy tune,
Echoed laughter, who cares to see?
In the dark, mischief blooms in June.

The fish tape dances in its bowl,
With fishy faces making a scene,
In silence, we find the funny role,
As we grin at the quirks in between.

In every corner, a chuckle hides,
Awaiting the brave to come near,
Silent secrets where humility bides,
We chuckle softly, still, but clear.

The Language of the Unheard

Words float like pollen in the air,
Unspoken thoughts, a comic spree,
A smirk, a wink, with utmost care,
Conversations of silliness and glee.

The coffee pot pants, brewing delight,
As sugar cubes tumble in despair,
What a sight! Wrong turns in the night,
Each stir creates a stampede flare.

The old chair groans like it knows a joke,
Underneath it, a surprise resides,
The dog lifts its head, eyes wide, awake,
Unheard laughter rolls, what it hides.

In silence, we roll on the floor,
Unexpected humor in muted array,
Here we chart laughter's unexplored,
The humor of nothing, in true display.

Silence Cradles the Moonlight

The moon peeks through with a wink tonight,
A giggle spills from a shadow's charm,
Stars chuckle low, a sight so bright,
While the night cradles its silent alarm.

In the stillness, socks dance bizarre,
A parade of solitude led by a shoe,
What a sight under the moonlight star,
Where whispers bloom, and giggles ensue.

An owl hoots like it's telling a tale,
Of whispers that tickle the sleepy air,
With quiet cheekiness, it won't fail,
As if humor's the currency we share.

In these hushed hours, fun can be found,
In the quiet, it plays hide and seek,
A laugh escapes, then circles around,
Under moon's watch—joy's little peak.

Into the Depths of Silent Shadows

In a house where echoes play,
A cat forgot to meow today,
The vacuum's roar, a clumsy beast,\nDistracts from the dog's sudden feast.

In corners where dust bunnies twirl,
They gossip about the fridge's whirl,
A sock slips past, on a joyful spree,
While the couch reclines, too tired to see.

The toaster hums a quiet song,
Whispers of bread that went wrong,
A mystery of crumbs left, forlorn,
Wishful tales of a muffin, all torn.

Yet laughter lingers, deep in the hall,
Where shadows dance at the silliest call,
In silence, there's much to hear and behold,
Strange tales of dishes, daring and bold.

Sheltered from the Roar

Under blankets piled so high,
Where secrets dwell and giggles sly,
The clock ticks loud, but no one cares,
For they're lost in laughter, sans pairs.

A plant pretends to take a nap,
While kids plot mischief, with a tap,
The phones buzz on with monotonous glee,
But in this cocoon, we're wild and free.

A cork pops, what a joyful sound,
In giggly corners, chaos is found,
The dishes tremble, on the rack,
As we plot the next snack attack!

Silence brings us closer, it's true,
As we share a snack, or two or three,
What's better than fun just out of sight?
Let's wrap it all up in sheer delight!

A Whisper's Journey in a Crowded World

In a jam-packed bus, I spot a seat,
But the whispers of snacks are hard to beat,
Someone sneezes, and chaos reigns,
While laughter erupts, and logic wanes.

A silent cat presides at the back,
That tiny paw waving, ready to attack,
Once a king, now in a feline dream,
Hoping for tuna, or ice cream, it seems.

The world outside, a blur of noise,
But inside, we fashion our little joys,
With just a whisper, a joke, or two,
Creating bubbles where laughter breaks through.

In the midst of all voices, we find our tune,
With humor as bright as a silvery moon,
Whispers connecting us, gentle, and warm,
In this curious bus, what a silly swarm!

Remnants of Laughter in Silence

In the attic, dust takes a leap,
Of forgotten moments, piled deep,
Old toys giggle, in shadows they play,
Recollecting the magic of yesterday.

A funny hat sits on a shelf,
Reminding us of an old, daft elf,
Who danced a jig in the middle of June,
It echoes still, like an old, silly tune.

With each quiet creak of the floor,
Laughter sneaks in, through the door,
Whispers of joy, a playtime reprise,
As memories bubble, under still skies.

So here's to the laughter, a playful surprise,
Found in silence, where essence lies,
In every corner, a jest, a tickle,
A world of joy, where it starts to giggle.

Shadows of Longing in the Quiet

In a corner, dust bunnies play,
Chasing whispers from yesterday.
A sock leaps high, then hits the wall,
As tumbleweeds of silence call.

Beware the chair that creaks at night,
It might just have a spine—what a fright!
Lost in thoughts that dance and sway,
While dreams forget they're meant to stay.

The teapot tells a joke or two,
While spoons laugh at the empty brew.
An echo sounds, a giggle here,
As the curtains wipe away a tear.

So if you feel a tickle near,
It's just the ghosts lending an ear.
Together they plot to shatter the calm,
With silly tricks and endless qualm.

An Abode of Echoing Thoughts

Here's a place where echoes bounce,
Off walls where all the dreams denounce.
A chair tried to explain to me,
That silence loves a cup of tea.

Half a plan in a book on the shelf,
Wondered if it could plan for itself.
The clock is giggling, hands stuck at noon,
While thoughts sneak out, like balloons in June.

A vase winks with its flowery cheer,
Unaware of the dust it needs to clear.
Each heartbeat sounds a drum of wit,
In a house where we mock the quiet a bit.

So if you knock, be sure to dance,
For echoes love a lively chance.
In shadows thick with humorous lore,
Find laughter hiding behind the door.

Stillness Cradles Night's Secrets

In the stillness, socks have fun,
Playing hide-and-seek with one.
The cat joins in with a sudden leap,
While the bed creaks secrets it's sworn to keep.

Moonbeams twinkle, casting spells,
As the toaster hums and chuckles, it tells.
A pillow whispers, "Why so glum?"
While shadows dance, and chairs succumb.

The clock ticks on with such a flair,
Trying to keep up with all this air.
Popcorn kernels sing in the bowl,
In this cozy corner, they take a stroll.

Now hold your breath, it's time to grin,
What's lacking here is a proper din!
Laughter rolls in, cradled tight,
As stillness giggles into the night.

The Comfort of Unvoiced Desires

On the shelf, a book sighs deep,
With lines it wishes, it could leap.
Cupboards close their teenage dreams,
While teapots spill their buzzing schemes.

The cat's opinion on global peace,
Is louder than a bowl of grease.
Cushions snicker, pointing the way,
Toward mischief that likes to play.

A window draws a breath from spring,
Bouncing thoughts on a silken string.
And floors whisper of wild delight,
As crickets compose symphonies at night.

So sit awhile, and hear the hush,
In every nook, where secrets rush.
For in this space, we let it pass,
Unvoiced desires dance with sass.

Murmurs in Empty Halls

Footsteps dance on polished floor,
But no one's here to hear the score.
Ghosts of gossip swirl around,
Yet the laughter makes not a sound.

Shadows play in dim-lit light,
Wrestling with the ghosts of night.
A squeaky door, a playful sigh,
Where did everyone else fly?

Spiders spin their webs of cheer,
While we're left with just our beer.
If walls could talk, they'd surely jest,
But they just stand, they take a rest.

Oh, the fun in no one's tale,
Boring moments set to sail.
When no one hears the silly quips,
It's just a joke that seems to slip.

Where Silence Gathers Dust

Dust bunnies hop on empty chairs,
A party where nobody dares.
The silence, thick like peanut spread,
Makes me wish that I had fled.

Whispers curl on the floor like curls,
While my mind does funny twirls.
What's that clatter? Just my shoes,
They're plotting moves I don't choose.

Laundry piles as high as dreams,
An audience of fading beams.
If only clothes could crack a smile,
I'd laugh with them for a while.

In this stillness, fears unmade,
Amusement waits in odd charades.
Here's to silence, cheers to dust,
In empty halls, we fight, we trust.

Echoes of a Distant Past

Echoes bounce on faded walls,
Like silly jokes in empty halls.
Nostalgia gives a goofy grin,
Reminding me of where I've been.

Old photos laugh from dusty frames,
Each capture shares its silly names.
The stories whispered, washed in time,
Are jumbled rhymes, a comic mime.

In the corners, memories peak,
With a wink or a jolly squeak.
Did that chair just chuckle loud?
Or is it just the lonely crowd?

Time flows like a wobbly dance,
In echoes, we find our chance.
To giggle, snort, and reminisce,
In spaces where we've shared that bliss.

The Solitude of Unspoken Words

Words float like balloons so bright,
Yet no one's here to hold them tight.
In this quiet, what a plight,
The jokes just fade, away from sight.

Scripts of laughter hang like art,
Waiting for a willing heart.
But silence loves to run the jest,
While whispers play a hidden quest.

Giggling echoes find their way,
Yet no one stops to laugh or play.
Each unspoken wish drifts by,
A lonely tumbleweed can't lie.

Here's to conversations missed,
In a quiet place that none have kissed.
I wish you were here to hear the puns,
But solitude plays with future runs.

Twilight Thoughts in a Pensive Light

In corners where the shadows dance,
I ponder why the spoons can prance.
The chairs conspire, they plot and scheme,
While I just sip my soda cream.

A clock ticks loud, with seconds bold,
It tells my secrets, or so I'm told.
The walls are listening, what a fright!
Yet here I sit, with sheer delight.

The cat is plotting, a grand escape,
While I debate, should I wear a cape?
Is silence golden, or just a tease?
Perhaps it's time for crackers and cheese.

So here I dwell in cozy gloom,
With sparkling thoughts that might just zoom.
In twilight's grip, where giggles peek,
I find my joy in whispers unique.

Unraveled Threads of Quietude

An empty space where socks imagine,
Planning parties that turn to raven.
The dust bunnies hop, a motley crew,
Inviting cobwebs for tea—how rude!

A curtain flutters, it can't hold still,
Pretending that it's shy, what a thrill!
I swear I heard the fridge just chuckle,
As midnight snacks dare to huddle.

Each creaky floorboard sings its tune,
The fridge hums back, like a lonesome moon.
In stillness, the spatula sways with glee,
Does it dream of a breakfast jubilee?

With laughter trapped in quiet corners,
I dance to echoes of playful mourners.
In thoughtful gaps where mischief swells,
I find the joy that silence tells.

The Stillness that Speaks Volumes

In a quiet nook where laughter hides,
The dust motes twirl like well-trained guides.
The sock drawer hums a wistful tune,
As I pretend to be a silly raccoon.

The chair creaks softly—an old friend,
Sharing whispers that never quite end.
The echo of silence, a quirky guest,
Declares the day's mischief—a raucous jest.

The cat yawns wide with a drowsy grin,
In this kingdom of calm, let the pranks begin!
With cushions plotting a soft rebellion,
What's truly quiet? It's a silly perception!

Yet in this hush, a chuckle may spring,
As nighttime cherubs begin to sing.
So I raise my glass to all things fun,
In the quiet chaos, where joy's never done.

Lanterns in the Lull of Night

Around the lamp, whispers lightly dance,
While gravity seems to give dreams a chance.
The fridge hums softly, an old serenade,
As spoons conspire, playing charades.

Beneath the shadows, the curtains play coy,
Turning peeks into giggles, oh what joy!
A lonely sock waves hello, quite absurd,
In this light of laughter—who needs a bird?

The stillness cradles pranks on its lap,
As I sip my tea, caught in a nap.
The clock rolls its eyes, a solemn face,
While I embrace this whimsical space.

With beams of moonlight tugging my heart,
Each moment whispers, "You're a part!"
So let's toast to the night with a clunky cheer,
Where silence and laughter dance in the clear.

The Unseen Threads of Quietude

In corners where whispers conspire,
Invisible threads play with fire.
A sock in the drawer starts to dance,
While the cat wonders, given the chance.

Dust bunnies giggle, what a delight,
As the fridge hums a tune late at night.
Yet even the walls must find their jest,
When the silence is louder than all the rest.

Remnants of Forgotten Laughter

Echoes of laughter float on the breeze,
Tickling the lampshades, teasing the trees.
A chair creaks, as if sharing a joke,
While the plants giggle behind their green cloak.

In the attic, old socks have a ball,
Pajamas parading, answering the call.
A tumble of giggles, oh, what a sight,
As slippers tango into the night.

A Tapestry Woven with Silence

Stitches of peace, woven so tight,
Draped over cushions, snug and polite.
Yet beneath it all, a tickle remains,
As the rug snickers at mundane chains.

A curtain sways, a wink and a smile,
Catching dust fairies, though only for a while.
Each thread a story, a chuckle, a sigh,
As the ceiling fans whisper, "Oh my, oh my!"

Still Shadows of Yesterday

Shadows of yesteryear linger and play,
In corners where boredom kept laughter at bay.
A table lamp winks, a sly little tease,
While the mirror reflects a ghost trying to sneeze.

The couch hides secrets, soft and absurd,
As pillows confide, without saying a word.
Chairs chat about who left crumbs on the floor,
In the silence that bubbles, who could ask for more?

Ghosts of Unvoiced Echoes

In corners where shadows dance,
Undone jokes find their chance,
A phantom giggles in the air,
As dust bunnies start to stare.

The walls might blush, or so I swear,
As laughter lingers everywhere,
Yet all they hear are muffled sighs,
From jokes that flew, but never rise.

A creaky floor plays peek-a-boo,
With gags that didn't make it through,
The ghost of humor floats around,
In silence where the laughs are drowned.

A tickle in the darkened room,
Where echoes dance like ghostly bloom,
Fallen from lips, they twist and twirl,
In the stillness, they swish and swirl.

Candles Flicker in the Dark

The candles flicker, dance and sway,
With silent pranks they choose to play,
A wink from one, a nod from two,
As if they know just what to do.

In shadows cast by waxen light,
Silly whispers take their flight,
They bubble up from deep within,
And laugh about what might have been.

A matchbox giggles, bright and proud,
While flames do stand, both tall and loud,
Yet in their glow, the wise confine,
All punchlines fall on shorter lines.

But watch them here in candlelight,
As echoes snicker, just out of sight,
For laughter lurks in every spark,
Where candles flicker in the dark.

The Weight of a Whisper

A whisper stumbles, trips and falls,
While silence sprawls across the walls,
It's heavy in its gentle curl,
Like a secret from a distant world.

It clutches tightly to the air,
As if it knows we wouldn't dare,
To let it go, to send it free,
Where all the laughter ought to be.

Yet humor drips like honey slow,
From lips that fear to make it glow,
The weight of giggles lost in grip,
As silent jokes prepare to slip.

So if you hear that quiet tease,
Just know it's there to bring you ease,
For laughter hides with whispers near,
And tickles silence, oh so clear.

Faceless Memories in the Dark

Faceless shadows, light is shy,
With secret laughs that weave and lie,
A chuckle here, a smirk or two,
In darkness where the memories flew.

They play hide-and-seek with our minds,
Like silly tricks that fate unwinds,
What's lost in gloom, we'd bring to cheer,
Those ghostly grins that persevere.

In corners deep, where whispers stroll,
Old tales bounce off the cellar's bowl,
A nudge, a wink, in playful haste,
Faceless laughs that swirl and taste.

So stumble over echoes past,
With memories that hold on fast,
In shadows, jokes await their spark,
Faceless fun within the dark.

Secrets Encased in Quietude

In the corner, dust bunnies dance,
A whispered giggle, a lost chance.
Chairs sway slightly, in tune with the breeze,
They hold secrets, and spare us with ease.

My socks debate in the still of the night,
Will they find mates or remain in flight?
Underneath blankets, whispers collide,
With mischievous laughter that could not abide.

Old pictures smirk on the wall's embrace,
As shadows play tag, with a comical grace.
In the closet, a shirt seems to pout,
Wishing for friends, it can't live without.

So tiptoe softly, you may hear a joke,
From the quietest corners, where silence bespoke.
Ears perk up, for the giggles unfold,
In the spaces where stories are joyfully told.

Forgotten Nooks of the Mind

In dusty corners, lost thoughts reside,
A pair of old shoes, waiting with pride.
The cat finds the warmth of a forgotten chair,
While memories hopscotch without a care.

Laughter echoes, trapped in a hat,
Where time takes a break, and naps like a cat.
An umbrella stands, with its story untold,
Of puddles and splashes, both timid and bold.

The fridge joins in, with a hum and a smile,
It's frozen adventures that stretch for a mile.
While leftovers chuckle, vying for fame,
A casserole whispers, "I've got a good name!"

Amidst the clutter, a dance can commence,
As thoughts tumble out, with curious suspense.
In forgotten nooks, creativity's found,
With silly imaginings that dance all around.

Subdued Melodies of the Unseen

Beneath the floorboards, a symphony plays,
Of creaks and of squeaks in mischievous ways.
A toaster hums softly, it's dreaming of toast,
While a kettle sings songs of warmth we love most.

The potted plant whispers of adventures at night,
As its leaves sway with laughter, matching the light.
A playful breeze flirts, tickling the air,
With secrets of mischief that happen with flair.

Curtains may giggle, ruffled with pride,
Hiding the chaos that's kept deep inside.
A wall clock rolls eyes, as the minutes drag slow,
Tick-tocking along, with a wink and a glow.

In shadows that frolic, the laughter ignites,
Each sound tells a story, in delightful bites.
So listen closely, let the whispers in,
The world's merry music will give you a grin.

In the Company of Shadows

The shadows conspire, in corners they meet,
With grins that unfold in a comedic retreat.
They play peekaboo under the flickering light,
Making merry mischief, from day into night.

A book rests ajar, with a wink from the shelf,
Offering tales of a whimsical self.
The lamp snickers softly, with warmth in its glow,
While dust motes dance, putting on a show.

Close the door gently, don't scare them away,
Or else they'll take flight, in a cloud of ballet.
A chair gives a sigh, of stories long past,
Where laughter was caught, but never could last.

So gather the giggles, and sip from the night,
In the company of shadows, everything's right.
For those hidden smiles, in the quiet behind,
Are the chuckles of life, so wonderfully kind.

The Still Reflection of a Forgotten Dream

A shadow lurks in the corner's gloom,
Whispers giggle, dispelling the doom.
A hat on a chair, with nobody near,
Laughs at my thoughts, tickles my ear.

Dust bunnies dance beneath the old bed,
A soft pillow cradles my weary head.
In this stillness, a joke takes flight,
Who knew absence could be so polite?

Outdated calendars mock my lost plans,
They flip through the years like awkward fans.
A light flickers, a wink from the dark,
Do ghosts throw parties? I hope there's a lark!

So I sit in my chair, sipping on tea,
In this quiet chaos, I'm blissfully free.
With every silence, a chuckle will bloom,
In the echoes of laughter, I find the room.

Crickets Sing in the Attic

A symphony starts where shadows entwine,
Crickets are crooners, sipping on wine.
They belt out tunes of the sleepless night,
While the moon winks at their jolly plight.

An old shoe watches, a casual guest,
It snickers softly, not wanting to rest.
The attic's a stage, with cobwebs for flair,
And jokes that float lightly, filling the air.

Dust motes are dancers, swirling in glee,
As laughter, unspoken, floats wild and free.
The joists are the audience, creaky and wise,
They clap for the crickets, eyes sparkling with surprise.

So here in the stillness, I chuckle away,
With my cricket friends making night feel like day.
Every chirp is a punchline, each pause a tease,
In the attic of dreams, we do as we please.

The Overgrown Garden of Restraint

In the corner, a flower speaks of its woes,
It's tired of waiting for someone who knows.
The weeds crack jokes, their laughter is bold,
While the garden sleeps under blankets of gold.

Chronicles grow in the mossy-spired walls,
Silly debates with no one at all.
A rogue tomato wears a crown made of dust,
While the sage nods wisely, it's all in good fun!

A fence stands guard, but it's brittle and weak,
Watching the antics of nature's own sneak.
In this jungle of whispers, laughter will bloom,
As I wander the pathways, sweet scent of the loom.

So here in the garden, where chaos still twirls,
I pick up the petals as their laughter unfurls.
Every last herb tells a joke, oh so grand,
In this overgrown haven, life's just a band.

A Symphony of Untouched Corners

Corners untouched, like secrets they keep,
A harmony hums where the shadows creep.
Dust settles softly, a blanket of grace,
As laughter erupts in this quiet place.

The chime of the clock ticks a funny beat,
Tickle-tock jokes that dance on my feet.
A portrait leans close, its eyes filled with jest,
As our silent gathering turns into a fest.

Beneath an old table, a dog snores away,
While whispers of fun in the woodwork play.
A curtain sways gently, a laugh on the breeze,
In this symphony's chaos, I find my ease.

So let silence linger, let echoes collide,
In these untouched corners, let joy be my guide.
With each breath I take, a chuckle will sound,
In this funny little world where peace can be found.

Echoes of Memory in a Quiet Room

In corners where dust bunnies dance,
Whispers of laughter, stuck in a trance.
Tickles of thoughts drift under the bed,
Where socks go to giggle, then sleep instead.

A chair creaks, making jokes from the past,
Old radios mumble, their signals quite fast.
Pictures are chuckling, framed on the wall,
Being a still life is a hard job for all.

The tablecloth whispers, it knows of the pies,
An apple long gone, oh how time flies!
Scents of banana and cocoa still play,
Even the curtains remember that day.

Yet here in this quiet, with echoes so bright,
Laughter still lingers, a ticklish delight.
In shadows that waltz, they hold time in glee,
A party of memories, just you and me.

The Still, Small Voice

Beneath the hush, the cat gives a shrug,
Turns back to nap, wrapped tight like a bug.
Amongst the soft sounds of silence's reign,
Even the fridge whispers, 'Snack time again!'

The clock has opinions, tick-tock it will chat,
Mocking my worries while slumped on the mat.
Each second it giggles, a tickle or two,
Guess it knows better what to do than you.

That old chair keeps cracking its bad dad jokes,
While I'm left wondering where humor provokes.
It chuckles at wrinkles now forming my face,
In this quiet kingdom, I'm losing the race.

But in this still space, even silence will choose,
To fill up the void with lighthearted blues.
And though there are times I may feel quite alone,
The whispers of laughter still hum on their own.

The Unwritten Canvas of Silence

With blank walls awaiting a splash of the odd,
An artist finds solace, a silent applaud.
Brush strokes of boredom paint shadows that peek,
In this empty gallery, the giggles are meek.

A wandering sock lost the mirth of its mate,
It holds quiet grudge against fate, not so great.
While secrets of giggles whoosh past like a breeze,
Traveling gently with whispers that seize.

The easel is grumpy, tired of its fate,
Bemoans the lost art of a silly debate.
Colors are waiting, with a wink and a sigh,
For a muse to arrive and paint laughter awry.

In this canvas of breath, colors may blend,
Each stroke could bring forth a very good friend.
So, let's scribble warmth in shades of delight,
And laugh through the silence, both day and night.

Faint Footfalls in the Memory's Hollow

Soft footfalls echo, tiptoeing light,
Ghosts of last Tuesday still hang out at night.
The fridge opens wide, it knows all the tricks,
As leftovers giggle, enjoy their antics.

In the hall, a soft shuffle, not footsteps at all,
Just the vacuum that's plotting a domestic brawl.
Each pile of dust is a critic, I swear,
Judging my cleaning with an attic's despair.

Whispers of parties in shadows still fade,
Where music and laughter had moments displayed.
They trip on old joy, like slipping on ice,
Each memory's joke is its own kind of nice.

So here in the quiet, while mischief will clamor,
I'll bop to the echoes, let laughter be my banner.
For though it seems empty, the whispers still play,
In the corners of silence, they dance night and day.

Wandering Through a Dreamscape of Stillness

In a place where whispers play,
The walls giggle every day.
Morning sneezes, sunbeams dance,
I trip on shadows, lost in chance.

Socks are missing, what a shame,
The cat is plotting, what a game!
Dust bunnies join the silent show,
With sock puppets about to glow.

Giggling curtains sway and tease,
I think the rug just threw a sneeze.
Furniture nods, an odd parade,
As I enjoy this grand charade.

Yet all the mirrors ponder me,
Reflecting jokes I cannot see.
Laughter hides in every crack,
In this stillness, I'll unpack.

In the Heartbeat of Hushed Hours

Tick-tock echoes, time stands still,
A cactus grins, it's got some skill.
The clock's a joker, runs amok,
With laughter hiding in the clock.

My teacup spills a funny tale,
As sugar cubes begin to sail.
A chair grumbles, needs a snack,
While I ponder how to unpack.

Raindrops giggle on the glass,
They tumble down as if in class.
The rabbit winked, my friend in plight,
In silent hours, we take flight.

Quiet giggles in the air,
Each moment whispers, teasing care.
In every heartbeat, calm and bright,
The funny stillness brings delight.

A House of Gilded Quietude

Underneath the golden glow,
A couch is plotting, don't you know?
The table's wobbly with delight,
As chairs gossip through the night.

A cookie jar holds secret dreams,
Filled with laughter, chocolate screams.
The lamp is winking, full of grace,
Illuminating this funny space.

Walls wear laughter's gentle hue,
As paintings hum a tune or two.
The rug, a clown, plays peek-a-boo,
In gilded stillness, joy breaks through.

Unexpected guests drop by,
A sock, a spoon, and one blue tie.
They share their tales in quiet jest,
In this house, we're always blessed.

www.ingramcontent.com/pod-product-compliance
Lightning Source LLC
Chambersburg PA
CBHW070311120526
44590CB00017B/2636